WINDMILL

LAOS

D0604975

Laos

A. Kamala Dalal

Martin Stuart-Fox and Viliam Phraxayavong, Consultants

NATIONAL GEOGRAPHIC

WASHINGTON, D.C.

Contents

Foreword

The Lao kingdom of Lan Xang was founded in 1353 by King Fa Ngum, but people had inhabited the area of present-day Laos for thousands of years. *Lan Xang* means "a million elephants." Since elephants were the tanks of ancient warfare, the name warned neighboring kingdoms that Lan Xang was a powerful state. In the early 18th century, however, Lan Xang was divided into three separate kingdoms, which in time were forced to pay tribute to Bangkok, in Siam. Under pressure from European governments, Siam (now Thailand) eventually gave part of its Lao territories to France, to become French Laos. After 60 years of colonization, Laos obtained full independence from France on October 22, 1953.

Although the independent Kingdom of Laos attempted to remain neutral, it was soon drawn into the Vietnam War, in which communists fought to overthrow the government, which was backed by U.S. forces. The country was heavily bombed and still suffers from the legacies of war. Unexploded bombs kill and maim people every year. After years of civil war, Laos became a socialist "people's democratic republic" on December 2, 1975.

Laos is very mountainous in the north and east, where it shares frontiers with China and Vietnam. To the west, the Mekong River forms most of its borders with Myanmar (Burma) and Thailand. To the south lies Cambodia. Many minority groups inhabit the highlands and plateaus, while most ethnic Lao farm the lowland plains along the Mekong and its tributaries. Laos is rich in minerals, timber, and water resources for hydroelectricity, which bring in substantial income. Laos is also a popular tourist destination.

Since Laos joined ASEAN (Association of Southeast Asian Nations) in 1997, it has been involved in many regional economic activities. It has become a land link rather than being landlocked. New roads and bridges have increased the flow of goods from China to Southeast Asia, and between Thailand and Vietnam. The government hopes that the efficient exploitation of its natural resources will enable Laos to achieve its goal of reducing poverty by 2020.

This book aims to inform young readers about the geography, wildlife, history, and culture of Laos, a country once known for its Cold War involvement but now a peaceful, modernizing, and developing Southeast Asian state.

▲ **A man waits on a dock of fish-tail boats, which are one of the quickest ways of getting around Laos on the Mekong and other rivers.**

Viliam Phraxayavong
Australian Mekong Resource Centre
University of Sydney, Australia

River *of* Plenty

THE MEKONG RIVER is vital to the Lao, the people of Laos. Laos is the only landlocked country in Southeast Asia, and the Mekong is its main source of water for people and livestock. The river system generates electricity at dams and waters fields to grow crops. It is a busy highway for cargo and passengers. Fish from the Mekong are an important part of the diet for the Lao people.

Nearly all of the Lao live by the Mekong. The river winds for more than 2,600 miles (4,180 km) from the frozen Tibetan plateau in China to the ocean in south Vietnam. Nearly half of its course lies in Laos. It flows through forested mountains in the north, between limestone cliffs in the heart of the country, and around more than 4,000 river islands in the south.

◀ **Lao fishers from Louangphrabang in northern Laos gather in their nets from the Mekong River at the end of the day.**

WHAT'S THE WEATHER LIKE?

Laos is a warm, tropical country. The hot air above the country contains a lot of moisture, which produces frequent rain showers. The heaviest rains arrive in May and last until September or October.

In the south of the country, temperatures in the lowlands can get as high as 104 °F (40 °C). They rarely gets lower than 50 °F (10 °C).

In the central mountains, it can get cold. The temperature drops to near freezing on the highest peaks in December and January.

The map opposite shows the physical features of Laos. Labels on this map and on similar maps throughout this book identify most of the places pictured in each chapter.

Fast Facts

OFFICIAL NAME: Lao People's Democratic Republic
TYPE OF GOVERNMENT: Communist
CAPITAL: Viangchan (local name); Vientiane (international name)
POPULATION: 6,677,534
OFFICIAL LANGUAGE: Lao
MONETARY UNIT: Kip
AREA: 91,429 square miles (236,800 square kilometers)
BORDERING NATIONS: Myanmar, Cambodia, China, Thailand, and Vietnam
HIGHEST POINT: Phou Bia 9,242 feet (2,817 meters)
LOWEST POINT: Mekong River 230 feet (70 meters)
MAJOR MOUNTAIN RANGE: Annam Cordillera
MAJOR RIVER: Mekong
MAJOR LAKE: Nam Ngum Reservoir

Average Temperature & Rainfall

Average High/Low Temperatures; Yearly Rainfall
LOUANGPHRABANG (NORTH):
96 °F (36 °C) / 80 °F (27 °C); 51 inches (131 cm)
VIANGCHAN (CENTER):
93 °F (34 °C) / 82 °F (28 °C); 67 inches (171 cm)
PAKXE (SOUTH):
95 °F (35 °C) / 64 °F (18 °C); 83 inches (211 cm)

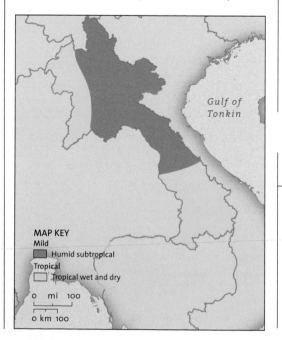

Gulf of Tonkin

MAP KEY
Mild
■ Humid subtropical
Tropical
□ Tropical wet and dry

0   mi   100
0   km   100

CHINA

Asia

Pacific
Ocean

LAOS

Indian
Ocean

MYANMAR

Muang Sing

VIETNAM

Ou

Ma

Xam Nua

JUNGLE VILLAGE,
page 15

ROAD WASHED
AWAY BY FLOOD,
page 15

Tha

Bĕng

L A O S

FISHERS,
pages 2, 6–7

Louangphrabang

Mekong

Xiangkhoang

*Plain of
Jars
Plateau*

Xiangkhoang

HILL TRIBE,
page 11

Gulf of
Tonkin

HIGH-SPEED
RIVER BOAT,
page 12

PADDY FIELDS,
page 13

*Nam
Khan*

Xaignabouli

GIANT STONE JARS,
page 12

MONKS IN
MOUNTAINS,
page 13

Ngum

+ *Phou Bia*
(Highest point in Laos)
9,242 ft
2,817 m

Kading

*Cammon
Plateau*

A n n a m   C o r d i l l e r a

RUGGED MOUNTAINS,
page 10

*Nam Ngum
Reservoir*

Mekong

Viangchan
(Vientiane)

Thakhek

Bang Fai

THAILAND

Ban Xénô

Savannakhét

Banghiang

Salavan

*Bolovens
Plateau*

Kong

Pakxé

Attapu

MAP KEY

⊛ National capital

● Selected city

□ Site

+ Elevation

Khone Falls

WATERFALLS,
page 14

Mekong River
(Lowest point in Laos)
230 ft
70 m

CAMBODIA

0   miles   100

0   km   100

Physical Map

▲ The mountains of Laos are made from limestone. Over the years, rain and river water have cut the soft rock into steep-sided peaks with many caves and deep valleys.

Between Water and Sky

Laos is a relatively little-known country, even though it is about the size of the U.S. state of Wyoming and is home to nearly seven million people. Laos has been isolated as a result of its geography. The country lies in the center of Southeast Asia and is largely cut off from its neighbors. Its borders with China in the north and Vietnam in the east are formed by steep mountain ridges. To the west, Laos is separated from Thailand by another natural frontier: the Mekong River. The Mekong flows into Cambodia to the south, but transportation between the two neighbors is blocked by one of the biggest series of waterfalls in the world. Because of these obstacles, centuries of travelers have chosen to go around Laos rather than through it.

HIGHS AND LOWS

Laos has many different groups of people who are associated with certain types of landscape. The Lao Loum people live in lowland areas. They make up about 70 percent of the country's population. However, most of Laos is high terrain that lies above 1,800 feet (600 m). The plateau regions are home to the Lao Theung, who make up 20 percent of the population. The final 10 percent, the Lao Soung, live among the rugged mountains. These three broad groups contain smaller ethnic communities. They include the Hmong people, who traditionally live in the hills. Instead of planting rice in paddy fields, the hill tribes clear trees from the hillsides to make way for crops. The government wants them to take up modern farming to stop damage to valuable forests.

▲ Hmong women and children wear traditional dress in a village high in the hills of Laos.

Walls of Peaks

Compared to other countries in Southeast Asia, Laos is a very uncrowded place. The population is relatively small. This is partly because almost three-quarters of the country is covered with mountains and forested hills that are too steep to live on. The major mountain range is the Annam Cordillera, which runs south from China and forms the main range dividing Laos from Vietnam. The mountain ranges are between 4,921 feet (1,500 m) and 8,202 feet (2,500 m) above sea level: only 10 percent of Laos is below 600 feet (182 m). Phu Bia, the tallest peak, is in the north. It rises 9,242 feet (2,817 m).

It is difficult and time-consuming to travel through Laos's hilly land. The country's first highway is still being built, and there are just a few miles of railroad

FAST BOAT UP A SLOW RIVER

For many Lao, traveling along the Mekong is the best way of getting from one end of the country to the other. In places, the river is more like a busy highway. Long, narrow boats are the most popular and cheapest form of transportation, but they are usually very slow. People in a hurry ride on a speedboat. These boats are much quicker—but also much more dangerous. Passengers wear earplugs to help block out the engine noise. The boats speed over the water, as passengers rely on the

▲ Crash helmets are essential safety gear on board the Mekong's high-speed passenger boats.

skill and knowledge of the driver to avoid hidden sandbanks and rocks.

connecting the capital, Viangchan (Vientiane), with Thailand. The roads through much of the countryside have not changed for centuries.

▼ The Plain of Jars is a flat area in central Laos that is dotted with huge stone jars. The man-made jars are centuries old, but no one is quite sure why they are there.

Plains and Plateaus

Laos has several plateaus, or high plains, that sit between the mountains and the Mekong. The largest is the Xiangkhiang in the center of the country, which includes the mysterious Plain of Jars. The Bolovens Plateau is located in the south, near the border with Cambodia. It covers 3,861 square miles (10,000 square km) and is an important farming area. Coffee, tea, and rice grow there. The plateau is

also famous for its pineapples and strawberries. Its deep soil makes it much more fertile than the Xiangkhiang Plateau.

The Khammouan Plateau is located at the country's narrowest point, where it is squeezed between Thailand and Vietnam. This plateau is made up of limestone hills, rivers, gorges covered in thick forests, and networks of caves.

The only true lowland in Laos is the floodplain along the Mekong River. This region is vital to the Lao. Farmers rely on the river's regular floods to cover the soil with a new layer of mud full of nutrients to grow rice and other crops. If the crops are not damaged by heavy storms, the Mekong Valley alone can grow enough food to feed the whole country each year.

▲ The center of Laos is a mixture of wide river valleys and steep hills.

▼ Laos's rice fields are divided by ditches that carry floodwater to the crops after heavy rain.

KHONE YOU BELIEVE IT?

As it flows toward the border with Cambodia, the Mekong River widens and its course is broken up by huge boulders. The water rushing over them forms a spectacular series of rapids and waterfalls called the Khone Falls. The Khone Falls are not as famous as some waterfalls in other countries, but more water runs over them than any other. About 2.5 million gallons (9.5 million liters) run over the Khone Falls each second—almost twice as much as the water that flows over Niagara Falls. The Khone are at their most spectacular after the summer rains.

The Khone Falls have played an important part in Lao history. It is impossible to get a boat past them, so the falls have acted as a barrier, effectively cutting off Laos from the ocean and busy ports to the south.

▲ The Khone Falls drop 70 feet (21 m) over a 6-mile (10-km) long stretch.

Waiting for the Rains

The upland plains are covered in what is called dry monsoon forest. As in cooler parts of the world, the trees here lose their leaves for part of the year. However, in Laos trees drop their leaves at hot and dry times of year, not in the cold of fall and winter.

A monsoon is a wind that changes direction twice a year. Between November and April, a hot, dry wind blows into Laos from China. In May the wind changes direction and brings moisture and rain up from the Indian Ocean. The rain increases steadily until July and August, when it is not unusual for it to rain for a

week without stopping, particularly in the south of the country. High on the Xiangkhiang Plateau, the rain creates fresh growth in the monsoon forest. Then the water gushes down small rivers to the Mekong and floods the fields along their banks.

▲ Local people try to bridge the gap after a flood has washed away the main road.

▼ A village nestles in monsoon forest in northern Laos.

Down in the Jungle

In the far south of Laos—a region known as the "panhandle" for its narrow shape—13 feet (4 m) of rain falls every year. The heavy rains are enough for the monsoon forest to be replaced by rain forest, or jungle. Here, the trees keep their leaves all year long.

Hidden Forests

WITH ITS SMALL POPULATION and almost impassable hills, Laos has many areas of natural habitat that have not been disturbed by people. When scientists reach remote jungles, they often make rare discoveries. In the late 1990s, for example, biologists found a whole new species of mammal. The soala is a small and secretive relative of cattle with long horns that lives only in Laos and over the border in Vietnam.

The ancient Lao forests are coming under threat, however. Illegal loggers have cleared tracks deep into the trees, making it easier for people to set up homes there—and to destroy the finely balanced habitat. It is not just the forest that is under threat. Many fish species in the Mekong River are also becoming rare.

◀ The red panda lives in the forests of northern Laos. This rare species is not actually related to the giant panda bear—it is more closely linked to raccoons.

NEW ARRIVALS

Laos is a tropical country, and the hot and humid weather makes it a perfect place for plants to grow. The thick forests provide homes for many animal species. Because the forests have been untouched for millions of years, the wildlife has evolved into a complex community containing a huge number of species. Each plant and animal has its own place in the system. If the system is disrupted, most species find it difficult to survive.

▼ Laos is home to several rare cats, including the tiger, clouded leopard, and fishing cat (below).

Species at Risk

Laos has a conservation problem. Several species that have become extinct in other parts of Southeast Asia have been found alive in Laos, such as the Indochinese warty pig. Despite this good news, these rare species will soon become completely extinct if their habitats in Laos are not protected. Laos's empty land, forests, and mines are very valuable to businesses in its more crowded neighbors, such as Thailand and China. Laos is a poor country and might have to sell its forests and other resources. This might help make the Lao better off, but it will not protect their wildlife. Species at risk include:

> Asian elephant
> Asiatic black bear
> Black gibbon
> Clouded leopard
> Eld's deer
> Fishing cat

> Giant Mekong catfish
> Irrawaddy dolphin
> Kouprey (cattle)
> Red panda
> Siamese crocodile
> Tiger

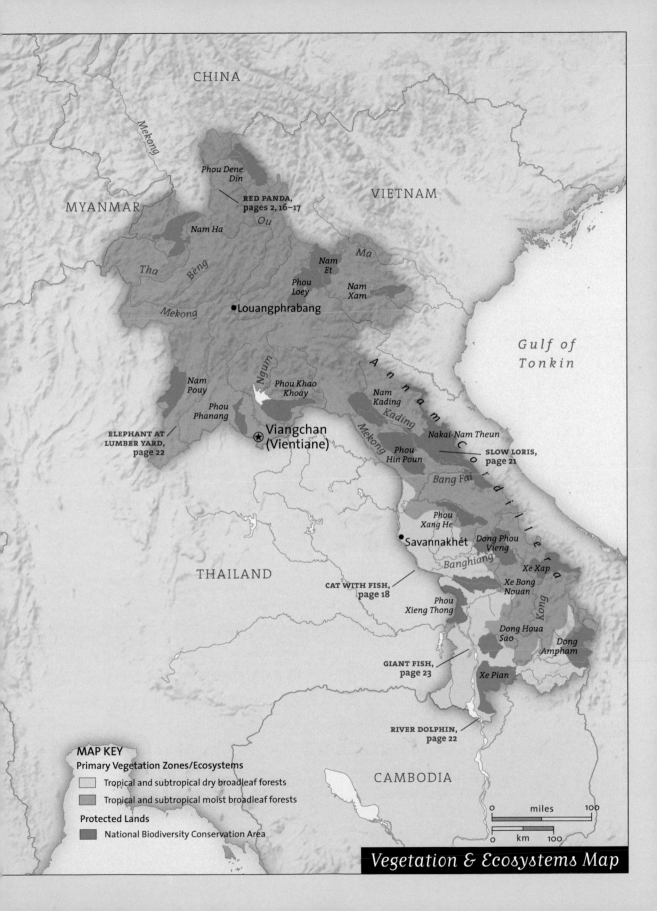

CHINA

MYANMAR

VIETNAM

Mekong

Phou Dene Din

RED PANDA,
pages 2, 16–17

Nam Ha

Ou

Ma

Nam Et

Tha

Beng

Phou Loey

Nam Xam

Mekong

●Louangphrabang

Gulf of Tonkin

Nam Pouy

Ngum

Phou Khao Khoay

Nam Kading

Annam

Kading

Phou Phanang

ELEPHANT AT
LUMBER YARD,
page 22

✪ Viangchan
(Vientiane)

Nakai-Nam Theun

SLOW LORIS,
page 21

Mekong

Phou Hin Poun

Cordillera

Bang Fai

Phou Xang He

THAILAND

●Savannakhét

Dong Phou Vieng

Banghiang

Xe Xap

Xe Bong Nouan

CAT WITH FISH,
page 18

Kong

Phou Xieng Thong

Dong Houa Sao

Dong Ampham

GIANT FISH,
page 23

Xe Pian

RIVER DOLPHIN,
page 22

CAMBODIA

MAP KEY
Primary Vegetation Zones/Ecosystems
  Tropical and subtropical dry broadleaf forests
  Tropical and subtropical moist broadleaf forests
Protected Lands
  National Biodiversity Conservation Area

miles
0   100

km
0   100

Vegetation & Ecosystems Map

Friendly Snakes

Snakes are a part of daily life in Laos. The country is home to many different kinds of snakes, including the deadly king cobra. People find snakes in the forests and fields, on the roads, or even in their homes. The snake that the Lao respect above all others is the nak. This mythical water serpent is believed to have special powers and is a symbol of death and rebirth. It is depicted in statues in Buddhist temples or carved on the prows of racing boats. It is always shown with its mouth open.

▲ Laos is home to one of the world's most dangerous snakes—the king cobra. This one is 14 feet (4.2 m) long; its bite could kill a human in less than an hour.

According to Lao legend, which contains Hindu and Buddhist stories, the nak drank all the world's water, causing a drought. Appealing to the gods for help, a king fired rockets into the sky. The god Shiva was pleased by the show and made it rain. Since then, the Lao have associated the nak with water. They believe the snake will also protect them from their enemies.

Some Lao think the nak really exists. They say that a photograph taken in World War II (1939–1945) shows U.S. soldiers holding a dead nak. Experts say that the creature was probably a large sea snake.

Tree Cover

In 1970, forests covered 70 percent of Laos, making it one of the most forested countries in the world. Just 30 years later, only 42 percent of Laos was still forested. The amount of forest is still falling.

▲ An area of Laos's lowland forest shows the scars of deforestation.

Deciduous hardwood trees, which are useful for lumber, grow on plateaus and slopes where there is not enough rainfall for jungle to grow. Beneath the

HOME OF SECRET SPECIES

The Nakai-Nam Theun is the largest protected area in Laos. It covers 1,428 square miles (3,700 square km) in the north of the country near the Vietnam border. The national park has rain forests, grasslands, and jagged mountain peaks. Recently it has been found to be the home of some of the world's rarest creatures.

Within the park's rugged forests live tigers, clouded leopards, rare wild Asian elephants, and Asiatic black bears—also known as moon bears for the pale crescents on their chests. More than 400 species of birds live in park. They include the endangered white-winged duck, crested argus, and greater spotted eagle. The most unusual resident is the soala, a very rare relative of sheep and cattle that looks more like a brown-and-white forest deer. The park is also home to other mammals previously unknown to science, including the giant-antlered muntjac.

▲ The slow loris lives in Nakai-Nam Theun. It is related to monkeys and is named for the way it creeps slowly through the branches, likely to go unnoticed.

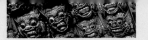

SPIRITS IN THE WATER

In southern stretches of the Mekong River lives a rare mammal—the Irrawaddy dolphin. The dolphin is found all the way from the South China Sea to the Khone Falls. The falls create a barrier that the dolphins cannot cross, but they are most often seen in small groups in the deep pool immediately below the falls.

The dolphin holds a special place in the hearts of the Lao. It is said that it is the only creature they will never eat. The Lao believe that the dolphins are the spirits of dead people. They also believe that the dolphins save people from drowning and protect them from the crocodiles that lurk in the river. Despite its special status, the Irrawaddy dolphin is under threat. One hundred years ago, there were thousands of dolphins in the Mekong. Today, there are fewer than a hundred in the wild. The dolphins have been killed off in large numbers by pollution and fishing nets.

▲ The blue-gray Irrawaddy dolphin is unusual because it has a snub nose.

▼ Most elephants in Laos are tamed. They are used to shift heavy loads, such as logs.

trees, the ground is covered with thick, bushy grass called *tranh*, or bamboo, and groves of wild banana.

The wetter lowland areas are home to rain forest. The tall trees form a thick layer of branches and leaves that prevents most of the sunlight from reaching the ground. The forest floor is relatively empty, with just a few orchids and ferns growing there.

Animal Magic

Laos has 200 species of mammals; a similar number of lizards, snakes, and frogs; and 700 species of birds.

However, the animals you are most likely to spot are livestock and pets. Laos was once named the Kingdom of a Million Elephants. Today, only a few elephants still live in the wild, but tame elephants are used to work in logging camps and to transport supplies through the forest. Another common mammal is the water buffalo. Most farmers have one to plow rice fields and to pull a cart. The buffalo wallow in rivers to keep cool.

Along the Mekong

The Mekong River has more than a thousand species of fish. Many, such as catfish, are a source of food for people in the south of the country. Food fish include a giant freshwater ray that can grow to 13 feet (4 m) long, including its spiny tail. The wetlands fed by river water around the Khone Falls provide nesting areas for birds, spawning grounds for fish, and one of the last habitats of the endangered Irrawaddy dolphin.

▼ Fishermen show off a huge Mekong catfish weighing 670 pounds (300 kg) and 8 feet (2.5 m) long. It is the world's largest species of freshwater fish.

Heart
of the
Country

THE TEMPLE ROOFS OF Louangphrabang are covered in gold tiles that sparkle in the sun. The city stands on a strip of land surrounded on three sides by water, with the Mekong to the west and the smaller Nam Khan River flowing around the north and east. This commanding position made the city the first capital of Laos. Although the capital has now moved south to Viangcha, Louangphrabang is still the religious center of the country.

Like modern Louangphrabang, for centuries Laos has been a calm place, cut off from its neighbors by rivers and mountains. However, in the 21st century, the country has become more connected to the outside world. Bridges across the Mekong now carry traffic into Laos from Thailand for the first time.

◄ **Boys run past the golden walls of Wat Mai, an ornate temple in Louangphrabang. The pictures on the wall tell the story of Buddha's life.**

THE LEGEND OF THE FIRST LAO

When exactly Laos became a country is something of a mystery. According to the most popular legend, the first Lao was called Khoun Borom. He was sent to rule over the land by the King of Heaven. Khoun Borom came to Earth sitting on the back of a white elephant. He came across a vine with two huge gourds dangling from it. He cut into them, and women, men, animals, and seeds poured out.

Among the people born from the gourds were Khoun Borom's seven sons. Each of them became ruler of a region of Laos, thus making seven small kingdoms. The oldest son, Khoun Lo, built his capital on the site of present-day Louangphrabang. Every king of Laos until the last one in 1975 has claimed to be descended from Khoun Borom.

▼ Most kings of Laos have lived in Louangphrabang beside the Mekong River. The last palace was built in 1904 and is now the national museum.

Time line

This chart shows some of the important dates in the history of Laos from when the north of the country was part of the Tai kingdom and the south was controlled by the Khmer civilization.

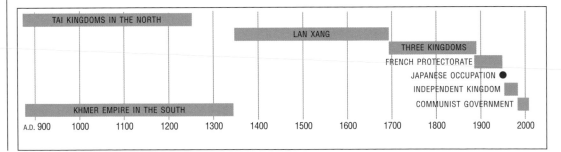

TAI KINGDOMS IN THE NORTH

LAN XANG

THREE KINGDOMS
FRENCH PROTECTORATE
JAPANESE OCCUPATION ●
INDEPENDENT KINGDOM
COMMUNIST GOVERNMENT

KHMER EMPIRE IN THE SOUTH

A.D. 900   1000   1100   1200   1300   1400   1500   1600   1700   1800   1900   2000

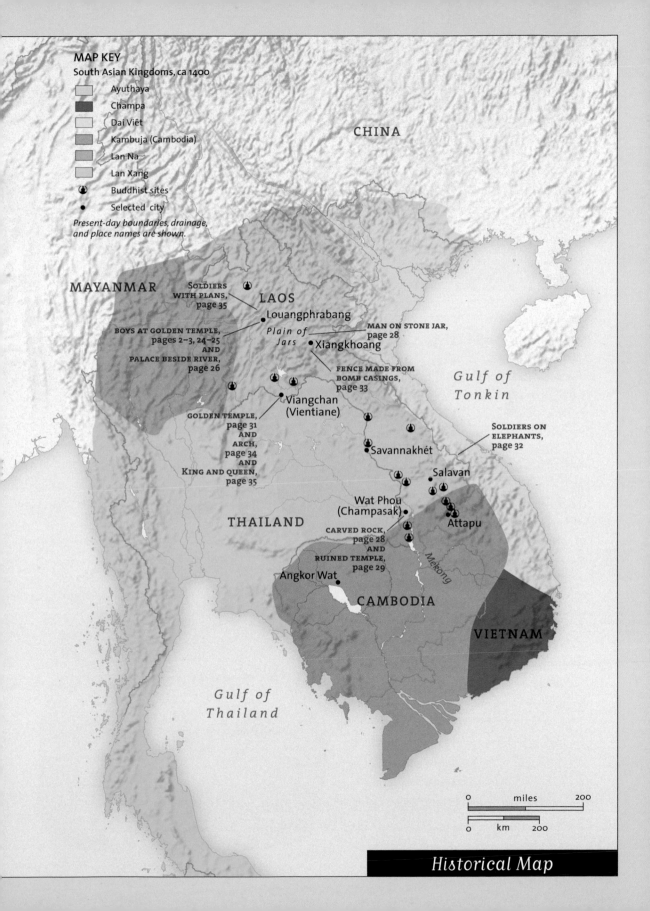

MAP KEY

South Asian Kingdoms, ca 1400

Ayuthaya

Champa

Dai Viêt

Kambuja (Cambodia)

Lan Na

Lan Xang

Buddhist sites

Selected city

Present-day boundaries, drainage, and place names are shown.

CHINA

MAYANMAR

LAOS

SOLDIERS WITH PLANS, page 35

Louangphrabang

Plain of Jars

MAN ON STONE JAR, page 28

BOYS AT GOLDEN TEMPLE, pages 2–3, 24–25 AND PALACE BESIDE RIVER, page 26

Xiangkhoang

FENCE MADE FROM BOMB CASINGS, page 33

Gulf of Tonkin

GOLDEN TEMPLE, page 31 AND ARCH, page 34 AND KING AND QUEEN, page 35

Viangchan (Vientiane)

Savannakhét

SOLDIERS ON ELEPHANTS, page 32

Salavan

Wat Phou (Champasak)

THAILAND

Attapu

CARVED ROCK, page 28 AND RUINED TEMPLE, page 29

Mekong

Angkor Wat

CAMBODIA

VIETNAM

Gulf of Thailand

0   miles   200

0   km   200

Historical Map

▲ Crocodile Rock in southern Laos is thought to have been used for human sacrifices about 1,500 years ago.

Early History

The first written records from Laos are from the 1500s. Before that time, our knowledge of early civilizations is limited to what archaeologists have discovered. We know the area of the lower Mekong Basin has been home to people for at least 10,000 years.

Experts think these first settlers were related to the Khmer people, who still live in Cambodia to the south. The arrival of the next group of people in Laos echoes some parts of the story of the first Lao, Khoun Borom. Beginning in about the eighth century A.D., people moved south from the Tai region, which is now the area of Yunnan in

GIANT MYSTERIES

The Plain of Jars is one of the most mysterious places in the world. About 600 immense stone "jars" cover a grassy plain in central Laos. The jars are at least 1,500 years old, but there are few clues about who made them and why. The jars appear to be carved from boulders. Legend has it that the jars were made to brew huge amounts of rice wine to celebrate a great victory in war. Another theory is that the jars were urns for storing the ashes of the dead. This idea is supported by the discovery of several underground burial chambers in the area.

▼ The largest urns are 7 feet (2 m) high and weigh 10 tons (9.8 tonnes).

southern China. Most of the lowland Lao (Lao Loum) are descendants of the Tai people. By the tenth century, Tai kings ruled a number of states in northern and central Laos—as in the Khoun Borom myth. The newcomers defeated the previous Lao inhabitants and drove them into the hills, where they became the Lao Theung (upland Lao). Khmer people continued to rule over what is now southern Laos.

▲ The ruins of Wat Phou are all that is left of a large temple-city in southern Laos. The city was an important center of the Khmer Empire in the 11th century.

Kingdom of a Million Elephants

Laos became a single kingdom for the first time when an exiled Lao prince named Fa Ngum returned from exile in neighboring Angkor in 1351. He led an army to unite the many kingdoms that covered what is now Laos. By 1353 Fa Ngum had made himself king of a new country called Lan Xang: the Kingdom of a Million Elephants.

The reign of Fa Ngum began an age of greatness for Laos. The kingdom stretched from the Red River of northern Vietnam into what is now northeast Thailand. Fa Ngum made Louangphrabang his capital and built many of its temples still in use today.

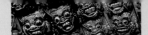

CREATING THE COUNTRY

Fa Ngum grew up in Angkor Wat, a huge Buddhist and Hindu temple complex in what is now Cambodia. As a result, Fa Ngum made Laos a Buddhist country. With the help of the Cambodian king, Fa Ngum succeeded in doing something that had not been done before. He united the Lao kingdoms of Champasak in the south with Xiangkhoang in the northeast and the kingdom of Muong Swa and its royal city, Louangphrabang, in the north. While Fa Ngum ruled, he expanded his country still further to include parts of southwest China, Thailand, and most of present-day Laos.

▼ Buddhist monks still worship at the Bayon, a temple at the heart of Angkor Wat. Even in Fa Ngum's time, the Bayon was already 300 years old.

In 1560, King Setthathirath moved the capital down the Mekong to Viangchan. After Setthathirath's death in 1571, however, the kingdom collapsed into disarray when invaders from Burma (now called Myanmar) took over.

Lan Xang did not regain its peace and prosperity until the reign of King Souligna Vongsa, the longest-ruling Lao monarch in history, (1637 until 1694). It was also during Souligna Vongsa's rule that Europeans first came to the country, in 1641.

Darker Times

Souligna Vongsa executed his only son for adultery, and so he died without anyone to take his place on the throne. The country split again into three kingdoms: Louangphrabang in the north, Viangchan in the center, and Champasak in the south. For the next 200 years, the region was repeatedly invaded by neighboring countries. In 1779, most of Laos was under Siamese rule (Siam is now known as Thailand). In 1827, the Lao rebelled. In revenge, the Siamese destroyed Viangchan and held the Lao king, Tiao Anouvong, as a prisoner in Bangkok for the rest of his life.

The French Take Over

The repeated invasions and wars made it easier for a European power to take over Laos. The French were looking for new colonies to compete with the British, who by then controlled Burma and India. The French had conquered Vietnam and were looking for a trade route into southern China. They wanted to use the Mekong River, but the Khone Falls blocked ships from sailing upriver. Instead, the French decided to try to make money from

▼ Viangchan's Pha That Luong stupa, or Buddhist temple, was built by Setthathirath in the 16th century but was destroyed 300 years later by the Siamese. The stupa was finally rebuilt in 1953.

▲ The Lao king signs a treaty with the French president to make Laos independent in 1953.

▼ French and Lao soldiers look for communist rebels as they patrol the jungle on elephants.

Laos's natural resources. In 1893, they forced the Siamese to withdraw from Laos to the western bank of the Mekong, which still forms the border with modern Thailand. The French then reunited the country into a single kingdom that was a little smaller than the original Lan Xang. It was the French who named the country Laos, which comes from the French name *les Laos*—the plural of *Lao*.

Unhappy Rulers

The French left the Lao king to rule his people, but a few hundred Frenchmen lived in the country to manage its businesses. The French soon decided that

SECRET TRAIL

During the Vietnam War (1964–1973), the U.S. Air Force dropped more bombs on Laos than the total of all bombs dropped on Europe by all sides during World War II. A U.S. bomber attacked Laos every eight minutes for nine years. The raids were kept secret because the United States was not at war with Laos. Their target was the Ho Chi Minh Trail, named for the North Vietnamese leader. This network of jungle tracks was used by the North Vietnamese to move supplies south to attack South Vietnam and its American allies. Most of the trail ran over the border in Laos, thus making that country a target for the bombers.

Plenty of evidence of the millions of bombs remains. Resourceful Lao have recycled shell casings to use as cattle troughs, water containers, and even pillars to support houses or barns. They grow vegetables in casings filled with soil. Large bomb craters have been turned into ponds for fish and ducks.

▲ This fence in Xiangkhoang is made from bomb casings. The people of Xiangkhoang took shelter from the bombs in a network of caves.

Laos was not much of a prize. The Mekong did not lead anywhere, and the steep mountains made it impossible to build mines and farms.

French rule came to an end in March 1945, during World War II (1939–1945). The Japanese took control of Laos, but their rule was very brief. By August, they had been defeated in the world war. In Laos, a struggle for power began between nationalist Lao leaders and the French, who hoped to take control again.

In 1953, the French made Laos fully independent, although French businesses still dominated the economy. Members of a movement called the Pathet Lao fought to get rid of them.

▼ The Pratuxai in Viangchan was built in 1969 as a monument to the Lao who died fighting the French. The name means "Arch of Triumph" in Lao, and the monument looks a little like the Arc de Triomphe in Paris, France.

A Secret War

Although Laos had gained its independence, other countries—especially the United States, France, and the Soviet Union—still competed to influence it. The Americans and the Soviets believed Laos was a key country in the Cold War, a political struggle between capitalism on the one hand and communism on the other. The United States backed the government run by the Lao royal family. However, the Pathet Lao began a violent rebellion against it. The rebels were supported by the communist government of North Vietnam, which was fighting a civil war against South Vietnam. The French and then the United States became allies of South Vietnam—and therefore enemies of the Pathet Lao. Operating in secret, U.S. forces attacked targets in Laos throughout the 1960s. By the time U.S. troops started to pull out of Vietnam in 1972, more than 750,000 Lao had fled their homes after fighting had spilled over the border from Vietnam into their country.

EXILE OF A ROYAL FAMILY

When the Pathet Lao seized power in 1975, King Sisavang Vattana (pictured with the queen) and his family disappeared. What happened to the royal family was kept secret for a long time. It was not until the late 1990s that their fate was revealed. They had been sent to a camp in the northeast of Laos but died soon after. No one is sure how the royals died, but it is probable that they became weak through lack of food and died from malaria.

Communist Control

In 1975 the Pathet Lao seized power. They got rid of the royal family that had ruled the country for more than 600 years and set up a communist state. The new government faced many problems. After years of war, most wealthy and educated Lao had left the country. There were few doctors and engineers left. Laos received money from the Soviet Union, but attempts to set up collective farms and to build factories failed. By the end of the 1970s, Laos was still a poor country of rice farmers.

▼ Pathet Lao personnel check construction plans as they begin to redevelop Laos after the 1975 revolution.

A Simple Life

LAOS IS ONE OF THE POOREST COUNTRIES on Earth. Many of its people have nothing more than the food they grow for themselves. But their tough life does not stop the Lao from being friendly, too. Their contentment stems from the country's long history of Buddhism, which teaches the Lao to seek happiness through a simple life.

Three-quarters of the Lao live in the countryside as farmers, and they have to work very hard to put food in the family cooking pot. However, families traditionally also share what food they have with Buddhist monks. The monks, in their saffron-colored robes, are seen across Laos. In the early morning the monks collect alms—gifts of food—from local people, who consider it an honor to help feed them.

◀ **A monk stands beside a giant statue of Buddha at Spirit City, a religious park near Viangchan. Although they look old, the park's statues were made from concrete in 1959.**

URBAN AND RURAL POPULATION

Most of the population of Laos lives in small rural communities close to the Mekong River or one of its many tributaries. The rest of the population, around 23 percent, lives in the three main cities. The largest city and capital, Viangchan, is home to just half a million people. Until recently, many of its major streets were unpaved. The other two big cities are Louangphrabang in the north and Savannakhet in the south.

Laos's population has doubled in the last 30 years to 6 million. One in ten Lao fled in the 1970s after the communists took power. Most of these emigrants now live in the United States, France, and Australia. Chinese and Vietnamese immigrants are coming to start new lives in Laos.

Common Lao Phrases

The Lao language—spoken by the Lao Loum—is similar to Thai. Here are a few common phrases. They are pronounced the way they are spelled.

Hello	Suh-bye-dee
See you later	Phop kan mai
Thank you	Kop jai
Yes	Men
No	Baw

▲ A Hmong village in the mountains of Laos is the only settlement for miles. The Hmong speak an unusual language thought to be related to Malaysian.

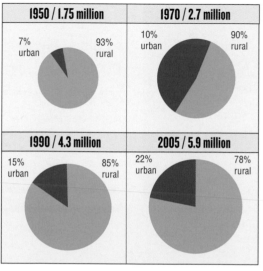

1950 / 1.75 million
7% urban — 93% rural

1970 / 2.7 million
10% urban — 90% rural

1990 / 4.3 million
15% urban — 85% rural

2005 / 5.9 million
22% urban — 78% rural

CHINA

miles 0 100

km 0 100

Phôngsali

VIETNAM

MYANMAR

Louangnamtha

FOOD STALL,
page 45

Xam Nua

Houayxay

MONKS IN LINE FOR FOOD,
page 41
AND
ORNATE SHRINE,
page 42
AND
QUIET STREET,
page 46
AND
SCHOOL BOYS,
page 47

Louangphrabang

Xaignabouli

Xiangkhoang

Gulf of
Tonkin

Phônhông

Viangchan
(Vientiane)

Pakxan

GIANT STATUE,
pages 3, 36–37
AND
TRAFFIC ON ROAD,
page 40
AND
PARADE,
page 43
AND
GRILLED FOOD,
page 44
AND
CROWDS AROUND TEMPLE,
page 44
AND
COLORFUL MOSAIC,
page 47

Thakhek

REMOTE VILLAGE,
page 38

Savannakhét

THAILAND

Salavan

Ban Phon

MAP KEY

Population of urban area

◼ Over 200,000

▲ 100,000 to 200,000

● 50,000 to 100,000

• Under 50,000

Pakxé

HOUSE ON STILTS,
page 40

Champasak

Attapu

People per
square mile

People per
square kilometer

Over 2500 | Over 1000

250–2499 | 100–999

26–249 | 10–99

2.5–25 | 1–9

Under 2.4 | Under 1

CAMBODIA

Country Life

To grow enough food each year, all the members of a Lao family need to work together. Children are expected to help their parents in the fields. Younger children do not have to do the heavy work in the rice fields. Instead they are left to watch the family's herd of cattle.

In the countryside families live together in small wooden houses. They have no running water or bathroom. All the water needed for drinking, cooking, and washing is carried from a river or stream, which is seldom far away.

▲ Houses near rivers are built on stilts to protect them from floods.

▼ The busy streets of Viangchan contrast with the quiet countryside.

City Living

The lives of Lao city dwellers are closer to the lives of people in Europe or the United States than to the lives of rural Lao. They tend to be wealthier. Adults work in offices or stores. Their children can attend school.

Being Kind

Around two-thirds of the Lao are Buddhists. Fa Ngum introduced the religion 650 years ago. The Lao follow a kind of Buddhism called Theravada, which is based on the idea of karma. People should behave well toward others in order to have a happy and lucky life themselves. However, the religion also teaches that many events are beyond a person's control, so people have to learn to accept their fate. This relaxed attitude toward life means the Lao are often seen as being laid-back.

Spirit World

Some Lao traditions pre-date the arrival of Buddhism, such as a belief in spirits, or *phii,* and have lasted into the 21st century. Buddhists believe in spirits linked to certain natural features, such as trees, rocks, and waterfalls. The celebration known as the Baci, popular in the lowland regions, is also older than Buddhism in Laos. The ceremony celebrates any important occasion, such as a marriage or birth. An artificial tree made from banana leaves and flowers is

▲ Monks stand in line in Louangphrabang to collect a cup of rice in their begging bowls. According to Buddhist teaching, it is the duty of families to provide food to the monks, who have no contact with their own homes or families.

MEDICAL EGG-XAMINATION

There are few doctors outside Lao towns, and when people get sick they rely on traditional methods to cure them. The Lao believe that bad spirits cause diseases. To diagnose a problem, traditional healers roll a raw egg over the part of the body that hurts. Then they break the egg and look at the yolk to find out which spirits are angry. To make the offended spirits feel better, the healers kill an animal as a sacrifice.

▼ Since the late 1990s, Pha Bang has been kept in an ornate shrine in Louangphrabang.

surrounded by offerings of food, often eggs and rice, both of which symbolize fertility. People gather around the tree and play music while prayers are read aloud. Guests tie cotton threads around each other's wrists as good luck charms.

A Precious Statue

Louangphrabang is an ancient city home to dozens of Buddhist temples, known as *wats*. It is also home to the most sacred statue in the country, the Pha Bang. The Pha Bang is made from gold and emeralds, but that is not what makes it special. The Lao believe that this ancient statue of the Buddha has special powers that protect their country. During Lao New Year celebrations in April, the statue is placed in a temple, where worshippers wash it.

The Pha Bang was given to Fa Ngum by the Khmers of Angkor. Legend suggests it dates back 2,000 years and was made in Sri

Lanka. Louangphrabang itself was named for the treasure. The city's name means "Royal Pha Bang."

There are many stories linked with the statue. Siamese invaders who stole it in the 18th century are said to have returned it to Laos because it brought Siam bad luck. Another rumor says that the statue in Louangphrabang today is a fake, and that the original was given by the Pathet Lao to their communist allies in the Soviet Union.

Musical Revolution

After years of isolation, the Lao are now enjoying their own pop music for the first time. Lao rap stars are the most popular. The band L.O.G. raps in Lao but is very popular in Thailand.

Rap is a long way from the traditional music and dance used to celebrate holidays. During religious festivals, people enjoy watching dancers perform stories from literature. The most popular show is the Lao version of the

NATIONAL HOLIDAYS

Laos has a lot of holidays, including four New Year's Days! The Lao celebrate January 1 along with the Chinese New Year, the Lao New Year, and the Hmong New Year. Many of their other holidays are part of the Buddhist calendar.

JANUARY 1	New Year's Day
JANUARY 6	Pathet Lao Day
JANUARY/FEBRUARY	Chinese New Year
MARCH 22	Day of the People's Party
APRIL 13–15	Lao New Year
MAY 20	Buddha Day
JUNE 1	Children's Day
JULY 18	Khao Pansa (Buddhist fast begins)
AUGUST 13	Lao Issara (Day of the Free Laos)
SEPTEMBER 22	Boun Ok Pansa (Buddhist fast ends)
OCTOBER 12	Day of Liberation
NOVEMBER/DECEMBER	Hmong New Year
DECEMBER 2	National Day

▲ Lao parade through Viangchan during the National Day celebrations in 2005, the 30th anniversary of the creation of the communist state.

Ramayana. This Indian epic was introduced to Laos by Khmer people who were Hindu. Dancers tour the country and give performances. The dancers are all men. Younger men play the female roles.

Rice with Everything

The staple food in Laos is sticky rice. It is eaten at every meal: there is even a sweet version for dessert. Rice dishes are flavored with spices and herbs, and eaten with river fish or chicken. People also eat beef, pork, and duck. Country villagers might add caterpillars and crickets to their food.

The French have left their influence on Lao food. City bakers bake croissants and long loaves called baguettes. The Lao eat their bread—and most other foods—with *nam pa*, a strong, spicy fish sauce.

▲ One of the things the French left behind in Laos was a love of frog meat, here grilled over charcoal (left).

▼ Thousands of people gather around Pha That Luang, the largest temple in Viangchan, during a festival in October.

KICKING KATAW

Kataw is very popular in Laos and across Southeast Asia. Played with a small, hollow ball made from woven bamboo, the game is a bit like volleyball, except that players may not use their hands. The aim is to hit the ball back and forth over a high net, although some people play without a net. Keeping the ball off the ground means lots of spectacular kicks and leaps. People can play anywhere; you even see kataw games on the grounds of Laos's temples.

▶ **The Lao national kataw team competed at the Asian Games. The game is very acrobatic at top levels.**

Taking Time Out

The Lao enjoy many unique sports, including rhinoceros-beetle wrestling. The beetles try to turn each other over with the long, hornlike spikes that stick out from their heads. Spectators bet on which beetle will stay standing the longest. The French introduced a ball game called *boule*, in which steel balls are thrown or rolled toward a target. The Lao know it as *petang*. The Lao

▼ **People grab a bite to eat at a stall on market day in Nam Tha.**

People & Culture **45**

WHERE'S THAT HOUSE?

It is perhaps just as well that only a quarter of the population in Laos lives in cities. The nation has one of the most complicated address systems in the world. To start with, most city houses are numbered twice. The first number shows which lot the building stands on. The second number shows its position on that lot. To make matters worse, there is no set way of ordering the numbers, so it can be difficult to know which is which.

If that is not confusing enough, only five cities in Laos have street names. Even then, street names often change as you move down the road. The best way to locate an address is probably to find out the nearest landmark.

▶ A quiet street in Louangphrabang.

are skilled petang players and won the gold medal at the 2005 Asian Games. Another popular sport is boxing, although in the Lao version fighters use both the hands and the feet to hit.

Away from the sports field, people might be smart to start collecting stamps. Stamps issued in Laos are among the most highly prized by the world's collectors. Lao stamps from the 1950s and 1960s are some of the most beautiful ever printed. The most valuable stamps feature the work of the French artist Marc Leguay. His stamps contain scenes of the Lao countryside and characters from myths.

Attending Class

In the past Lao boys were educated in Buddhist monasteries. When the French controlled Laos, they set up schools for boys and girls. Many lessons were taught in French, and as a result older Lao still speak that language.

▲ This artwork of polished glass and stones inside a temple in Viangchan tells a traditional story.

When the communists took power in 1975, they stopped teachers from using French. All lessons were in Lao. The new government also cut illiteracy. By 1985, it claimed that around 80 percent of adults could read and write. Over the next decades, as more children were taken out of school to work, the figure fell. Today 68 percent can read, and English has replaced French as the main foreign language taught in schools.

School is required for children between ages six and fourteen. However, it is hard to enforce the law among the scattered rural villages. Even today, many country children still do not go to school. Those who do often have to live at the school during the week, because it is too far to travel from their homes.

▼ A pair of schoolboys learn to write at a school in the countryside.

Cut Off from the World

TO A FAMILY OF LAO FARMERS, the state of the world economy may not seem important. They live in a wooden hut surrounded by rice fields, probably close to a river. The family grows rice and perhaps keeps a few cows or ducks. They do not buy very much, although they may exchange spare food with neighbors for things they need.

In the 1980s and 1990s, the Lao economy was cut off from the world. It remained relatively stable, because it was not affected by the ups and downs of international trade. However, the lack of trade meant that Laos stayed very poor. The country has now opened itself up to foreign business, and the quality of life is slowly rising. Still, 75 percent of the people have less than $2 to spend each day.

◀ **A woman plants rice seedlings in a muddy field while her children sit in the shade of bamboo baskets.**

ONE OF THE FEW

Laos was once ruled by a king. The throne was passed down from each ruler to his eldest son. In 1975, communists took over and changed the system. At that time, many countries had communist governments. Today, most of them have switched to democracy. Laos is one of just five communist states left, along with its neighbors Vietnam and China. The government still tries to control all political activity but does allow private businesses. The country is run by a single political party: the Lao People's Revolutionary Party.

Trading Partners

Laos imports a lot more than it exports. Its largest exports include lumber, coffee, electricity (generated by dams), tin, copper, and gold. Laos has to import manufactured goods such as machinery, vehicles, fuel, and kitchen appliances.

Country	Percent Laos exports
Thailand	42.1%
Vietnam	9.5%
China	4.0%
All others combined	44.4%

Country	Percent Laos imports
Thailand	68.8%
Vietnam	5.6%
China	1.3%
All others combined	24.3%

▼ A soldier salutes the Lao (left) and communist (right) flags on the 30th anniversary of communist rule.

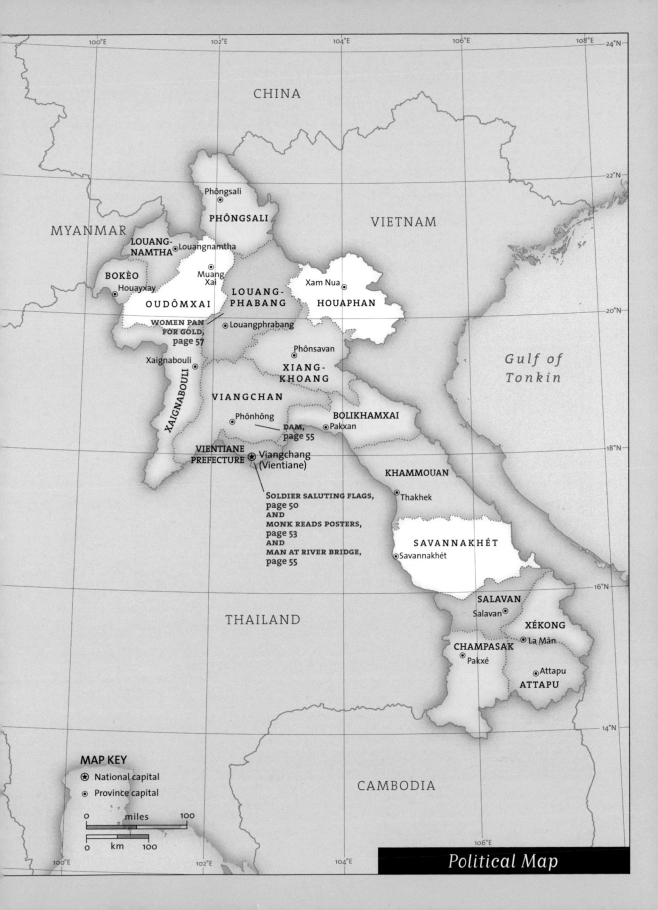

CHINA

100°E 102°E 104°E 106°E 108°E 24°N

22°N

MYANMAR

Phôngsali
PHÔNGSALI

VIETNAM

LOUANG-
NAMTHA
Louangnamtha

BOKÈO

Houayxay

Muang
Xai

Xam Nua

OUDÔMXAI

LOUANG-
PHABANG

HOUAPHAN

20°N

WOMEN PAN
FOR GOLD,
page 57

Louangphrabang

Gulf of
Tonkin

Xaignabouli

XIANG-
KHOANG

Phônsavan

VIANGCHAN

Phônhông

DAM,
page 55

BOLIKHAMXAI

Pakxan

18°N

VIENTIANE
PREFECTURE

Viangchang
(Vientiane)

KHAMMOUAN

SOLDIER SALUTING FLAGS,
page 50
AND
MONK READS POSTERS,
page 53
AND
MAN AT RIVER BRIDGE,
page 55

Thakhek

SAVANNAKHÉT

Savannakhét

16°N

SALAVAN

THAILAND

Salavan

XÉKONG

La Mân

CHAMPASAK

Pakxé

Attapu

ATTAPU

14°N

MAP KEY

National capital

Province capital

0   miles   100

0   km   100

CAMBODIA

100°E 102°E 104°E 106°E

Political Map

Economic Failure

Laos is a one-party state. The communists have been in power since 1975. They tried to run the country on strict communist lines by taking control of all the farmland and factories in the country and organizing workers into groups called collectives. However, the plan did not work. The collective farms did not grow enough food, and people either starved or moved out of the country. The government has now abandoned this approach and allows people to own their own farms and to run private businesses. It has also

HOW THE GOVERNMENT WORKS

All public officials in Laos are members of the Lao People's Revolutionary Party (LPRP). The head of state is the president, who is also the leader of the LPRP. The current president is Lieutenant General Choummali Saignason. He was elected in June 2006, along with a vice president. These officials are both elected to serve a five-year term by members of the National Assembly. The head of the government is the prime minister, Bouasone Bouphavanh. He serves with four deputy prime ministers. The prime minister is nominated by the president and elected by the National Assembly, also for a five-year term. The 115 members of the National Assembly are elected by the people of Laos every five years. Only people approved by the Politburo—a powerful body in the LPRP—are allowed to run for election. The main court in Laos is the People's Supreme Court. The judges are chosen by the National Assembly.

LAO PEOPLE'S REVOLUTIONARY PARTY		
EXECUTIVE	LEGISLATIVE	JUDICIARY
PRESIDENT	POLITBURO	PEOPLE'S SUPREME COURT
PRIME MINISTER	NATIONAL ASSEMBLY	LOCAL COURTS

allowed foreign companies to invest in Laos and has stopped paying for state-run factories that cost more money to run than they earned.

Despite these economic changes, the political system is still controlled by the communist party. People with different ideas about how to run the

▲ Election campaigns are quiet affairs in Laos. Here, a monk examines posters about people running for election to the National Assembly.

A CONTROVERSIAL PLAN

Over the last 50 years, Laos has lost many of its forests. There are several reasons why the forest is being cut down, including both legal and illegal logging. However, the government mainly blames the highland Lao for their method of clearing the forests to grow food. The government has forced many highlanders, especially Hmong, to move to lowland areas. Not everyone agrees with this plan. Critics say it is just a way for the government to control Laos's ethnic minorities. The conflict has led to terrorist attacks on government targets.

▲ A Hmong family builds a temporary hut in a new lowland home.

country are not allowed to run for office.

Business Boom

The early 21st century was a boom time for Laos. There was a huge growth in wealth and trade. Partly, that was because Laos was so poor during the 1990s that it had a lot of room to improve. Despite the boom, a third of the Lao cannot survive without help from the government or charities.

Helping Hands

Laos still has very little infrastructure. It has only just started building its first railroad, it has a very basic road system, and rural villages do not have TVs or cell phones. The country needs money from abroad to improve highways and communications networks.

Laos has a history of foreign aid that dates back to the 19th century, when the French bankrolled the expansion of its cities. During the early days of its communist states, Laos received most of its money from the Soviet Union. However, that ended when the Soviet Union broke up in 1991. Today, China is Laos's main foreign partner.

MAKING CONNECTIONS

I n 1994, Laos's isolation ended with the opening of the Friendship Bridge across the Mekong River. The bridge links the capital of Viangchan with neighboring Thailand. The bridge has Laos's only railroad. It also has a four-lane highway, which forms the starting point of a modern road network that is still being built. However, the link is not that simple: Cars drive on the left in Thailand but drive on the right in Laos. A system of stoplights at the Lao border crossing allows traffic to swap from one side of the road to the other safely. In 2007 a second bridge across the Mekong was opened near Savannakhet.

▲ The Thai–Lao Friendship Bridge has become the busiest trade route in Laos.

River Power

For centuries, foreigners came to Laos to try to tame the fast-flowing waters of the Mekong River. That proved impossible until the end of the 20th century, when construction technology was finally able to dam some of the Mekong's tributaries. The energy produced by dams on the Mekong river system is more than enough to power Laos. The extra is sold to its neighbors. There are currently four dams in Laos. The largest is on the Nam Ngum River north of Viangchan.

▼ As well as being the nation's largest power plant, the Nam Ngum Dam is also popular with day-trippers who take boat trips on the large lake formed behind the dam.

INDUSTRY

The untouched forests of Laos are a valuable source of lumber. Laos needs to protect this natural resource from illegal loggers who smuggle teak and other hardwoods to Vietnam. Other important natural resources include gold, copper, and aluminum ore. Mining is becoming a large part of the Lao economy. Foreign companies are investing large sums to reach the valuable gold and copper that is hidden deep inside the mountains. Previously the lack of a road network in the hills made mining there impossible.

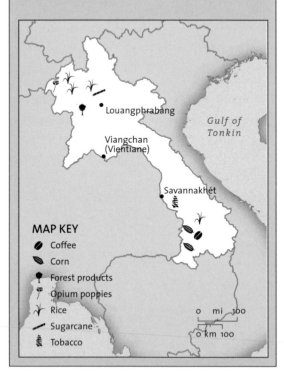

Louangphrabang

Gulf of Tonkin

Viangchan (Vientiane)

Savannakhét

MAP KEY
- Coffee
- Corn
- Forest products
- Opium poppies
- Rice
- Sugarcane
- Tobacco

0   mi   100

0   km   100

Several more dams are planned, including the Nam Theun II Dam in Khammouan province, which is being built at a cost of $1.1 billion, paid for mainly by France and Thailand. Thailand will buy 90 percent of the electricity made by the dam. Dam building does cause some problems, however, including more deforestation.

Opening the Doors

A major growth area for the Lao economy is tourism. After Louangphrabang was added to the United Nations list of World Heritage Sites in 1995, the city became much better known. In 1990, only 14,400 tourists visited Laos. Today up to a million tourists arrive each year. They are drawn by the country's amazing landscapes and a way of life that cannot be seen anywhere else.

Growing

Lao farmers all live and work on just 10 percent of the country's total land area. The rest of the land is too steep for growing crops. Rice farming in the Mekong Valley depends a lot on the weather. Heavy rains can destroy the crop and leave a family without food. The few crops grown for sale, rather than to support the family, include corn, wheat, cassava, soybeans, and cotton. At higher elevations farmers grow crops such as tea, coffee, tobacco, and spices.

▲ Lao girls pan for tiny amounts of gold mixed with the silt carried in the water of the Mekong.

Good Times Ahead?

Although the lives of most Lao are getting better, the country needs to work hard to ensure that it keeps getting wealthier. The communist system makes Laos a stable place, but it gives ordinary people little say in how the country is run.

One big problem facing the country is corruption. Officials take illegal payments from businessmen in return for mining and logging licenses. This damages the natural resources—forests, rivers, and minerals—that are the country's greatest economic asset. Many Lao want to balance economic growth with preserving and protecting the environment.

▼ A farmer checks his ducklings for illness. Laos is one of the countries suffering from a deadly bird flu, which experts fear may spread to humans.

Add a Little Extra to Your Country Report!

If you are assigned to write a report about Laos, you'll want to include basic information about the country, of course. The Fast Facts chart on page 8 will give you a good start. The rest of the book will give you the details you need to create a full and up-to-date paper or PowerPoint presentation. But what can you do to make your report more fun than anyone else's? If you use your imagination and dig a bit deeper into some of the topics introduced in this book, you're sure to come up with information that will make your report unique!

>Flag

Perhaps you could explain the history of Laos's flag and the meanings of its colors and symbol. Go to **www.crwflags.com/fotw/flags** for more information.

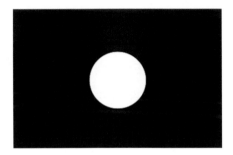

>National Anthem

How about downloading Laos's national anthem and playing it for your class? At **www.nationalanthems.info** you'll find what you need, including the words to the anthem, plus sheet music for it. Simply pick "L" and then "Laos" from the list on the left-hand side of the screen, and you're on your way.

>Time Difference

If you want to understand the time difference between Laos and where you are, this Web site can help: **www.worldtimeserver.com**. Just pick "Laos" from the list on the left. If you called someone in Laos right now, would you wake them up from their sleep?

>Currency

Another Web site will convert your money into kips, the currency used in Laos. You'll want to know how much money to bring if you're ever lucky enough to travel to Laos: **www.xe.com/ucc**.

>Weather

Why not check the current weather in Laos? It's easy—go to **www.weather.com** to find out if it's sunny or cloudy, warm or cold in Laos right now! Pick "World" from the headings at the top of the page. Then search for Laos. Click on any city. Be sure to click on the tabs below the weather report for Sunrise/Sunset information, Weather Watch, and Business Travel Outlook, too. Scroll down the page for the 36-Hour Forecast and a satellite weather map. Compare your weather to the weather in the Lao city you chose. Is this a good season, weather-wise, for a person to travel to Laos?

>Miscellaneous

Still want more information? Simply go to National Geographic's World Atlas for Young Explorers at **http://www.nationalgeographic.com/ kids-world-atlas**. It will help you find maps, photos, music, games, and other features that you can use to jazz up your report.

Glossary

Adultery being unfaithful to a husband or wife.

Buddhist a person who follows the teachings of Buddhism.

Civil war when two or more groups living in the same country fight each other for control of all or part of the territory.

Climate the average weather of a certain place at different times of year.

Colony a region that is ruled by a nation located somewhere else in the world. Settlers from that distant country take the land from the region's original inhabitants.

Communism a system of government where a single political party rules a country with the job of ensuring that wealth is shared equally among all people.

Culture a collection of beliefs, traditions, and styles that belongs to people living in a certain part of the world.

Economy the system by which a country creates wealth through making and trading products.

Endangered at risk of dying out.

Executed killed as punishment for a serious crime.

Exported transported and sold outside the country of origin.

Geography the study of Earth's surface.

Habitat a part of the environment that is suitable for certain plants and animals.

Hindu a follower of Hinduism, a religion founded in India that involves the worship of many different gods and spirits.

Imported brought into the country from abroad.

Infrastructure the basic utilities provided by a country's government, such as bridges, roads and railroads, telecommunication systems, schools, and hospitals.

Limestone stone made from the remains of seashells and other chalky substances.

Monarchy a system of government that is headed by a king or queen.

Monsoon a wind that changes direction throughout the year. When the monsoon blows from the land to the ocean, the weather is dry.

Nationalism a belief or political movement that celebrates a certain nation or country. Nationalists believe that their government should not be controlled by people from another country.

Plateau a high, flat area.

Reign the period when a king or queen rules a country.

Rural a region that has large areas of country-side and farmland. Rural areas have fewer people than urban places.

Species a type of organism; animals or plants in the same species look similar and can only breed successfully among themselves.

Treaty a written agreement between two or more countries. Treaties are made to end wars or to organize trade.

Tributary a small river that flows into a larger one.

Bibliography

Brittan, Dolly. *The People of Laos.* New York: PowerKids Press, 1997.

Laos—In Pictures. Minneapolis, MN: Lerner Publications Co., 1996.

Mansfield, Stephen. *Laos.* New York: Marshall Cavenish, 1998.

http://news.bbc.co.uk/1/hi/world/asia-pacific/country_profiles/1154621.stm (general information)

http://www.aseansec.org/ (official Web site of the Association of Southeast Asian Nations)

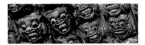

Further Information

NATIONAL GEOGRAPHIC Articles

O'Neill, Thomas. "The Mekong—A Haunted River's Season of Peace." NATIONAL GEOGRAPHIC (February 1993): 2–35

Web sites to explore

More fast facts about Laos, from the CIA (Central Intelligence Agency): https://www.cia.gov/library/publications/the-world-factbook/geos/la.html

This Web site contains information on all of the provinces of Laos. Click on the map to find out more: http://www.visit-laos.com/where/index.htm

This site is full of general information about the country: http://www.laos.co.uk/

The Pak Ou caves are in cliffs above the Mekong River near Louangphrabang. The caves, used as a Buddhist temple, are full of statues. Take a look at this hidden wonder at: http://www.laostravel.info/Cave/index.htm

Louangphrabang is one of the holiest cities in the Buddhist world. This video from UNESCO, the United Nation's cultural organization, is a good introduction to the unique city: http://whc.unesco.org/en/list/479/video

The Plain of Jars is certainly a mysterious place. Learn about some of its secrets at: http://www.traveladventures.org/continents/asia/plainofjars.shtml

This radio documentary tells the stories of the bomb hunters who are searching Laos for the unexploded

bombs that have covered the country since the U.S. bombing campaign in the 1960s and '70s. Take a listen at: http://www.pri.org/world/asia/bomb-hunters-laos.html

Listen to some Lao pop music and watch videos of the most famous stars at: http://laomusic.la/music.html or http://www.laopress.com/index.html

See, hear

There are many ways to get a taste of life in Laos, such as movies and music. You might be able to locate this:

Vientiane Times
The only English-language newspaper printed in Viangchan is also available on the Internet: http://www.vientianetimes.org.la

Index

Boldface indicates illustrations.

Credits

Picture Credits

Front Cover – Spine: Certe/Shutterstock; Top: David Ball/Corbis; Low Far Left: Redlink/Corbis; Low Left: Bohemian Nomad Picture Makers /Corbis; Low Right: W. E Garrett/NGIC; Low Far Right: Redlink/Corbis.

Interior – Corbis: Atlantide Phototravel: 47 lo; Bettmann: 32; Christophe Boisvieux: 15 up; Michele Falzone: 46; Owen Franken: 44 up; Vincent Gautier: 21 up, 33, 43, 50; Michel Gounot: 12 up; Jeremy Horner: 42 lo; Suthep Kritsanavarin: 23 lo; Jose Fuste Raga: 4 left, 36-37; Reuters: 45 up, 57 lo; Paul A. Souders: 40 lo; Chaiwat Subprasom: 53 lo; Sukree Sukplaang: 53 up; Robert Patrick/Sygma: 55 lo; Steven Vidier: 34; Barbara Walton: 22 up; Nick Wheeler: 28 up, 29, 44 lo; Micahel S. Yamashita: 6-7, 57 up; Frans Lemmens/Zefa: 2, 15 lo; Getty Images: Hoang Dinh Nam: 55 up; NGIC: Stanley Breeden: 18 lo, 21 lo; Paul Chesley: 5, 30, 47 up, 54; WE Garrett: 4 right, 10, 11 up, 13, 35, 38 lo left, 40 up, 45 lo, 48-49; Martin Gray: 31; Taylor S. Kennedy; 3, 16-17; Mattias Klum: 20; W. Robert Moore: 26; Alison Wright: 11 lo, 28 lo, 41; Michael S. Yamashita: 3-4, 14 up, 22 lo, 24-25; Shutterstock: 59:

For information about special discounts for bulk purchases, contact National Geographic Special Sales: ngspecsales@ngs.org

For more information, please call 1-800-NGS-LINE (647-5463) or write to the following address:

NATIONAL GEOGRAPHIC SOCIETY
1145 17th Street N.W.
Washington, D.C. 20036-4688 U.S.A.

Visit us online at www.nationalgeographic.com/books

Library of Congress Cataloging-in-Publication Data available on request
ISBN: 978-1-4263-0388-3

Printed in the United States of America

Series design by Jim Hiscott.
The body text is set in Avenir; Knockout.
The display text is set in Matrix Script.

Front Cover—Top: Buddhist monks walk past Pha That Luang, Viangchan. Low Far Left: Stalls in a night market, Louangphrabang; Low Left: Water buffalo; Low Right: Akha woman; Low Far Right: A fisher casts his net at Paxke

Page 1—A girl in the traditional dress of a Lao hill tribe; Icon image on spine, Contents page, and throughout: Masks

Produced through the worldwide resources of the National Geographic Society

John M. Fahey, Jr., *President and Chief Executive Officer;* Gilbert M. Grosvenor, *Chairman of the Board;* Tim T. Kelly, *President, Global Media Group;* John Q. Griffin, *President, Publishing;* Nina D. Hoffman, *Executive Vice President, President of Book Publishing Group*

National Geographic Staff for this Book

Nancy Laties Feresten, *Vice President, Editor-in-Chief of Children's Books*
Bea Jackson, *Director of Design and Illustration*
Jim Hiscott, *Art Director*
Virginia Koeth, *Project Editor*
Lori Epstein, *Illustrations Editor*
Stacy Gold, Nadia Hughes, *Illustrations Research Editors*
R. Gary Colbert, *Production Director*
Lewis R. Bassford, *Production Manager*
Nicole Elliott, *Manufacturing Manager*
Maps, *Mapping Specialists, Ltd.*

Brown Reference Group plc. Staff for this Book

Volume Editor: Tom Jackson
Designer: Dave Allen
Picture Manager: Sophie Mortimer
Maps: Martin Darlison
Artwork: Darren Awuah
Index: Kay Ollerenshaw
Senior Managing Editor: Tim Cooke
Children's Publisher: Anne O'Daly
Editorial Director: Lindsey Lowe

About the Author

A. KAMALA DALAL is a British-born writer with an Indian father and an English mother. She has traveled extensively in South and Southeast Asia and in China, and has written many nonfiction books for children.

About the Consultants

MARTIN STUART-FOX is Emeritus Professor of History at the University of Queensland, Australia. He has written six books on Laos, and others on Cambodia and China's relations with Southeast Asia. Professor Stuart-Fox is a Fellow of the Australian Academy of the Humanities. He regularly returns to Laos to conduct research.

VILIAM PHRAXAYAVONG is an associate of the Australian Mekong Resource Centre of the University of Sydney, Australia. His book *The History of Aid to Laos (1950–2005)* will be published by Silkworm Books, Thailand, in early 2009. He was director of international economic cooperation at the Ministry of Economic and Social Planning of the Royal Lao Government for 10 years (1965–1975) and later worked at the Department of Irrigation in the Ministry of Agriculture for four years (1981–1984). Dr. Phraxayavong is compiling an annotated bibliography of materials (in English and Lao) on development in Laos which summarizes key points and outlines materials useful to people studying Laos.

Time Line of
Lao History

B.C.

ca 500 An ancient Mon–Khmer people make huge stone "jars" that are sometimes larger than a person; today the jars are found throughout central Laos.

A.D.

ca 500 Thai speakers emigrate from southeastern China into northeastern Laos.

ca 800 The Laws of Khoun Borom document the teachings of the mythical father of the Lao, Khoun Borom.

ca 900 The Khmer kingdom of Cambodia grows to include large areas of present-day Burma, Laos, and Thailand.

ca 1100 Khmer King Suryavarman II builds two large reservoirs at Wat Phu, a temple at the base of Lingaparvata.

1300

1353 King Fa Ngum establishes the kingdom of Lan Xang and unites most of modern-day Laos.

1373 Fa Ngum is overthrown by his son.

1400

1478 Vietnamese forces led by Le Tanh Thong invade Lan Xang, conquer the capital at Luangphrabang,and occupy the kingdom for a year.

1500

1558 Burmese forces take control of Chiang Mai and destroy much of western Lan Xang.

1560 King Setthathirath moves the capital to Viangchan, to protect Lan Xang from Burmese invasions and bring it closer to Thai protection.

1569 Burmese armies invade Lan Xang and occupy Viangchan until King Setthathirath forces the invaders out.

1571 Setthathirath is killed during an attempted invasion of Cambodia. Lan Xang comes under Burmese control.

1600

1637 Souligna Vongsa claims the throne of Lan Xang and unifies the kingdom. He builds many temples and schools and increases the wealth of the country.

1641 A Dutch merchant becomes the first European to make contact with Lan Xang.

1694 Souligna Vongsa dies without an heir; struggle for control breaks out.

1700

1707 After Vietnamese and Siamese (Thai) forces have been fighting for control of Lan Xang for ten years, the kingdom is broken up into three parts: Luangphrabang, Vieng Chan, and Cham Pasak.

1763 Burma launches a vast and devastating attack on Luang Phrabang, the Siamese kingdom based at Ayutthaya, and other Lao areas.

1778 Siamese general Chaophraya Chakri conquers Viangchan and takes its most precious sculpture, the Emerald Buddha, back to Bangkok.